ROGER PIERANGELO
GEORGE A. GIULIANI

CREATING CONFIDENT CHILDREN

USING
POSITIVE
RESTRUCTURING
IN YOUR
CLASSROOM

Research Press
2612 North Mattis Avenue • Champaign, Illinois 61822
(800) 519-2707 • www.researchpress.com

Composition by Jeff Helgesen
Cover design by Precision Graphics
Printed by Bang Printing

ISBN 0–87822–428–9
Library of Congress Control Number 2001096111

To my wife, Jackie; my two children, Jacqueline and Scott; my parents; my sister, Carol; and my brother-in-law, George

In memory of Billy Smyth, a truly extraordinary person and one of the most gifted men I have ever known

R. P.

To my wife, Anita, and my two children, Collin and Brittany, who give me the greatest life imaginable

G. A. G.

Contents

Acknowledgments

I wish to thank the students and parents of the Herricks Public Schools. It has been my pleasure to know and work with them for the past 28 years. Their insight, feedback, and support have been invaluable in the writing of this book. My gratitude also to Helen Firestone, who was instrumental in my career and always believed in me, and to John Okulski, a great individual and unique educator.

R. P.

I want to express my gratitude to my parents, George and Carol Giuliani, who always made going to school a rewarding experience by giving me the self-confidence to believe I could succeed at anything I did.

G. A. G.

Our appreciation also goes to our friends at Research Press—especially to Ann Wendel and Karen Steiner—for their support and encouragement for this project.

R. P. and G. A. G.

Introduction

Creating Confident Children: Using Positive Restructuring in Your Classroom aims to help teachers, parents, and other professionals develop a foundation of confidence in children. Without confidence, children's learning, retention, and thinking may be greatly diminished. Positive Restructuring, a developmentally appropriate and organized approach, can help educators promote confidence in their students, thus ensuring greater capacity and motivation for learning.

Teachers face problems every day with children who are resistant or unmotivated, have fears of failure, avoid handing in work, are unwilling to participate, and so on. Many times, these behaviors are treated without an understanding of their underlying causes and of the role of children's lack of confidence in their own abilities. When children lack confidence, numerous secondary symptoms occur, in turn straining both their self-esteem and the patience of their teachers.

Teachers are well aware of how wonderful the classroom environment can be for children who already have a sense of confidence. They participate, are motivated, have a positive outlook, are willing to venture out, will try new things, and enjoy doing their work and learning. Often the difference between students who act this way and succeed in school and those who do not is a matter of perceptions: Students who do well have high levels of confidence, and students who do not have low levels.

We have seen many programs that attempt to build self-esteem and confidence by having children repeat positive statements about themselves. When these children do poorly in school, their parents also often reassure the children of how bright and capable they really are. The first thing these children do is compare these messages with what they know about their actual performance. This situation is like telling children they are great tennis players when they have never hit a ball! Without repeated real-life experiences of success, children do not find much encouragement in these words.

For children's perceptions of their abilities to change for the better, their actual performance must improve. Once children have experienced success and developed a certain degree of confidence, actual behavioral outcomes can also change. This book, then, is about how to build children's confidence by structuring the classroom for success.

- Chapter 1 explains why students' confidence is the foundation for learning, describing the importance of self-esteem and positive teaching style.

- Chapter 2 discusses Positive Restructuring, the methodology for enhancing student confidence, and describes how one teacher used a "Confidence Month" to ensure his students' success.

- Chapter 3 outlines possible causes for low self-confidence originating in academic, environmental, psychological, social, and other areas of students' lives.

- Chapter 4 tells teachers what student behaviors to look for to recognize students with low levels of confidence.

- Chapter 5 concerns the effects of teaching style, for better or worse, on students' level of confidence.

- Chapter 6 discusses classroom practices that teachers can put into effect right away to improve students' self-esteem and self-confidence.

- Chapter 7 details the use of "Success Bank Accounts," a whole-class method for improving self-confidence by tracking and rewarding student successes.

- Chapter 8 describes a number of general principles that teachers and parents can follow to help build children's confidence.

The book concludes with Parent News Notes to explain the program and help parents build their children's self-confidence at home.

CHAPTER ONE

Confidence: The Foundation for Learning

Many theories of learning take into account the function of the brain and how information is processed. Further, most theories of learning assume that a foundation exists on which to build. Although the success of human learning is a result of many factors coming together at one time, one factor is essential—namely, confidence. Confidence is not magical, nor is it difficult to understand. It is merely the result of repeated successful experiences. If we think back to our confidence level the first time we rode a bicycle versus the 50th time, we see how experience and, more important, success increased our confidence. This principle relates to our every enterprise.

Without successful experiences on which to draw, children will not believe that they are capable of doing well. Telling children they are bright, special, unique, capable, and so on can only go so far. Without actual experiences to validate these words, the words have little or no meaning. Children build on what they see, which in turn affects what they feel. When it comes to building confidence in the classrooms of America's schools, we may tend to let children down.

SELF-ESTEEM

Self-esteem refers to how we feel about ourselves. High self-esteem, feeling good about ourselves, allows us to keep failure situations in proper perspective. Whether a situation is perceived as a learning experience or a failure depends on our level of self-esteem. Children as well as adults vary greatly in their degree of self-esteem. We all feel more confident on some days than others, and feeling low self-esteem from time to time is not a problem. However, success is important for the growth of positive feelings about oneself, and a continuing pattern of low self-esteem is worthy of concern.

The feeling of self-esteem is expressed in the ways people behave. Parents and teachers can easily observe children's self-esteem by seeing what they do and how they do it.

More often than not, children with high self-esteem . . .

- Feel capable of influencing others' opinions or behaviors in a positive way
- Are able to communicate feelings and emotions in a variety of situations
- Behave independently
- Approach new situations in a positive manner
- Exhibit a high level of frustration tolerance
- Take on and assume responsibility
- Keep situations in perspective
- Communicate positive feelings about themselves
- Are willing to try new situations
- Feel that whatever happens is a direct result of their own behavior or actions
- Feel a sense of power over their environment

More often than not, children with low self-esteem . . .

- Make self-derogatory statements
- Exhibit a low frustration tolerance
- Easily become defensive

- Listen to others' judgments rather than heeding their own
- Resist new situations and experiences
- Blame others for their failures and problems
- Have little feeling of power or control
- Lose perspective easily (blow things out of proportion)
- Avoid situations that create tension
- Are unwilling to reason and discuss
- Feel anything that happens to them is the result of fate, luck, or chance

To fully understand self-esteem, you must consider the factors involved. Self-esteem is high when children experience satisfaction associated with the following feelings.

Feeling connected

A child feels good relating to people, places, and things that are important to her, and others approve of and respect these relationships.

Feeling unique

A child acknowledges and respects the personal characteristics that make him special and different, and he receives approval and respect from others for those characteristics.

Feeling powerful

A child uses the skills, resources, and opportunities she has to influence the circumstances of her own life in important ways.

TEACHING STYLE

The power a teacher has to influence children's self-esteem and self-confidence is a theme of the film *Mr. Holland's Opus*. For 30 years, Mr. Holland taught music at a local high school, only later recognizing the positive impact he had on his students' lives. As educators, we have seen this phenomenon ourselves:

Many of our former students have written cards and letters indicating how we were positive role models in their professional development. Ironically, these students rarely—if ever—gave any indication during their schooling of how important we really were to them.

Positive Teaching

The teaching styles of excellent teachers are very different. Yet across these different teaching styles, most tend to take into account students' need first to feel confident about themselves through successful experiences. For example . . .

- Mrs. S. is a fifth-grade teacher with a great sense of humor. She is not afraid to joke with her students because she feels confident about maintaining control. Mrs. S. provides numerous positive experiences each day for the students in her class, and she structures assignments and projects for success. She is keenly aware of every student's individual needs and abilities, and she always gears her requirements accordingly. As a result, the children in her class love school, and the parents experience positive feelings about their children's school performance.

- Mr. C. is a teacher who treats his classroom like his home and his students like guests, always making them feel welcome. He treats his students with respect and provides assistance so that all students feel good about themselves. His attitude is reflected in the positive way his students treat one another.

- Ms. T. is a first-grade teacher who loves children. She realizes how fragile children are at this age and prepares lessons and experiences that never result in failure. She constructs her assignments on many levels so everyone gets to the end with success. She is more interested in her students' feeling good than in being the authority.

- Mr. B. has been a baseball coach for 20 years. He expects a lot from his players and will only accept a team approach to the game. He makes his players work very hard and follow the rules, and he tolerates no nonsense. Yet his players idolize him because he is fair and treats everyone with respect.

Negative Teaching

Just as positive teaching can reinforce students' confidence, negative teaching can undermine it. If you have ever had a negative teacher, we are sure that you remember the name, grade, and year you had this individual. And we are also pretty sure that you still harbor bad feelings about your experience.

Many times it is not children who fail school, but schools who fail children. The problem in a great number of classrooms is that students do not have enough successful experiences to build a foundation of confidence. Moreover, some teaching styles actually devalue students and prevent success. Some actual examples follow.

- Mr. D. believes that his third graders need to be prepared for life at the age of 9. Mr. D. provides guidance with criticism, intimidation, hard tests, and threats. Many of his students get sick in the morning, have trouble falling asleep, hide bad grades from their parents, and lie about their school performance.

- Mrs. W. feels that public humiliation is a good technique to motivate children to become stronger. So she asks children to stand up in front of the class for several minutes if they fail a test or do not do their homework.

- Ms. L. is a fifth-grade teacher who believes that students learn best by doing a great deal of work. As a result, Ms. L. gives 3 hours of homework a night. Many of the parents of students in Ms. L.'s class see this as an indication of how much their children are learning. However, many of these parents have to work along with their children, finish assignments for them, or get into nightly arguments about homework.

- Mrs. T. never smiles. She sees first grade as a serious matter. She teaches the same way she has for 24 years and, by being rigid, unapproachable, and punitive, makes learning stressful. Her children are always on edge because they are afraid to make a mistake and get her angry.

- Mr. M. is a second-grade teacher. Mr. M. gives difficult tests from the first day of school to let his students know who is the boss. He requires students to memorize a great deal and tests them often, frequently humiliating them in public if they answer incorrectly. He says he expects a certain number of failures and that he is preparing his students for the real world.

Examples of both positive and negative teaching styles abound in schools. The luck of the draw—and sometimes the involvement of parents—determines the teachers a child may have and the educational road the child will take. Each road may have a very different destination and may affect a child's future more than we realize. One year with a great teacher or one year with a destructive teacher can affect a child for the rest of his life.

If we assume that confidence is a crucial foundation for success, then confidence in the classroom should be the basis for academic success. Unfortunately, many classrooms do not provide enough repeated successful experiences, given in a controlled and orderly fashion, to allow children even to begin feeling confident of their abilities. Although classrooms that do not stress success may work for children who already feel confident when they come to school, they fail children who have never developed a foundation of success. Attempting to add to the knowledge base of children who have not yet developed the foundation of success is like trying to build a house on sand.

Confidence and self-esteem do not occur naturally in all children. They are qualities that must be nurtured. As a teacher you have a unique opportunity to influence your students' futures directly in the classroom and to work with parents to help them build children's confidence at home. You may not realize it as it is happening, but the way you teach may determine whether or not your students develop enough confidence to build continued academic success.

CHAPTER 2

Building Confidence Through Positive Restructuring

Many books available today offer teachers ideas, "gimmicks," "projects," and the like for building confidence and self-esteem. However, in these books the responsibility for developing self-confidence is assumed to reside solely within the child. Rarely do such books take into account the contributions of teaching or parenting style toward a student's feelings of self-worth, nor do they consider the student's actual experience of success. Offering a student numerous confidence-building exercises when that student only experiences failure is useless. As Dr. Onkar Ghate states:*

> Genuine self-esteem . . . consists not of causeless feelings, but of certain knowledge about yourself. It rests on the conviction that you by your choices, effort and actions have made yourself into the kind of person able to deal with reality. It is the conviction based on the evidence of your own volitional functioning that you are fundamentally able to succeed in life and, therefore, are deserving of that success.

*From *Say No to the Self-Esteem Pushers* by O. Ghate, 1998, Charleston, SC: Post and Courier.

Positive Restructuring involves rethinking the classroom to ensure that all students experience success. According to this theory, it is a mistake for educators to expect children with low self-confidence to absorb anything when most of their energy is going into self-protection in the form of the kinds of behaviors associated with low self-esteem listed in chapter 1: low frustration tolerance, defensiveness, blaming others for their own failures and problems, and so forth. For these children, the energy available for building a positive sense of self is limited, and failure experiences contribute to an ongoing negative cycle.

There is no doubt that Positive Restructuring—consciously and systematically helping students achieve success—requires a great deal of work. Some educators and administrators may see Positive Restructuring as unrealistic in the regular classroom. If they believe this, then what they are really saying is that it may be too much work to build children's confidence. That would be a very sad statement about the educational system.

As educators, we have an obligation to question teaching that frustrates children, makes them feel like failures, reinforces their inadequacy, promotes negative self-worth, exposes them to ego-deflating experiences, or promotes adult egos at the expense of student success. More pragmatically, if we are unable to defuse negative energy and redirect students toward positive experiences, then our job as educators becomes almost impossible. In short, the long-term benefits of working to develop students' overall sense of confidence greatly outweigh any initial expenditure of time and effort.

A great teacher can make students feel good about themselves, but their sense of self-worth may depend on the personality of that teacher. Many times, students' confidence diminishes when they are confronted with a different teacher who may not be as focused on success. All teachers need to evaluate the experiences they offer children on a daily basis.

Do the experiences promote confidence and build internal feelings of success that carry over from year to year, even when children are not experiencing great teaching?

PRINCIPLES OF POSITIVE RESTRUCTURING

Positive Restructuring makes a number of assumptions about teaching and learning. Teaching according to these assumptions requires consistency, genuineness, and discrimination on the part of teachers. No single suggestion will have long-lasting effects; a combination of techniques will have greater impact. Teachers and parents should keep in mind that many factors not within their control (e.g., peer group, school success or failure, perceptions) will also contribute to children's degree of self-confidence. However, the role of teachers and parents is a crucial one and can offset difficulties in other areas.

Teachers also need to be aware of certain principles of Positive Restructuring theory that apply to the concept of confidence building in children.

Every child is capable of being successful.

Students need to believe from the start that they are capable of success in some or all areas of school. What prevents many students from embracing this belief is the amount, type, and level of work presented to them, coupled with a definition of success based on group comparison (e.g., tests, grade-level standards, etc.). When group comparison is the benchmark for success, failure will always occur. But what purpose is really served by student failure? Failure serves only to reduce students' confidence, set them off from other students who score better, increase their feelings of inadequacy and resentment, expose them to parental anger and frustration, and encourage avoidance.

Some—perhaps most—schools practice what we call "triage education," based on the belief that a certain number of casualties are acceptable. If our medical system tolerated a high death rate, there would be public outcry. Schools tend to accept failure and point to unmotivated, troubled youth or poor parenting as the cause. Although these factors play a part, we must also look at the role of the delivery system used by schools.

Every child has potential that may not have been exhibited up to this point.

It is unrealistic to insist that schools provide the opportunity for all children to express their true potential. What is realistic is to expect schools to offer students the opportunity to realize their potential in some areas. Areas of potential include but are not limited to the following:

- Creative potential (visual arts, music, drama)
- Intellectual potential
- Physical potential
- Academic potential
- Social potential

It is important for schools to explore all areas to see where a child's true potential lies. Although it is true that potential may not be expressed until a student is a certain age, it is never too early to start exploring. As educators we sometimes forget that not everything good about a child always happens in school and that success in areas other than the academic adds to a child's self-confidence both in and out of school.

Confidence is the necessary foundation for feeling good about oneself and one's ability.

Like adults, children need to learn that building confidence is a process that develops from successful experiences and not overnight.

There is hope for all students, even those who may not have felt successful up to this point.

Failure forces a child into a box labeled *inadequate*. Coaxing a child out of this box is not easy, but a child can become self-confident if teachers recognize the difficulty the child has faced previously and nurture the child's hope that change is possible.

As the teacher, you are in charge and know what you are doing.

Conveying a strong leadership message to children gives them structure and the knowledge that someone knows how to get the most out of them. Being a good "lifeguard" is crucial for children to feel secure and confident.

Once students have confidence, they will be motivated to try other experiences.

Success breeds success. A child who lacks confidence will have a very small "safety zone," or area in which she feels adequate or comfortable. Unfortunately, small safety zones are associated with the following characteristics, among others:

- Unwillingness to try new experiences
- Giving up easily
- Rigidity
- Low frustration tolerance
- Self-doubt
- Social isolation
- Avoidance
- Intolerance of others

Discuss with students the limitations of a small safety zone and the excitement of expanding beyond it. If you like, use the metaphor of living in a closet versus living in a mansion.

It takes time to build confidence.

Like growing taller, confidence grows in individuals at different rates. It is important for students to realize that some of their peers will gain confidence more quickly than they, but that they will gain confidence on their own timetable. Achieving a sense of self-confidence is not a competition but a process that can unfold in all children.

Feeling confident and good about oneself is always better than feeling inadequate.

Children who lack confidence learn over time to perceive their feelings of inadequacy as a "normal state"—normal for them, at least. They must learn that feeling good about themselves is better than feeling inadequate, even if inadequacy is the only feeling they know. With work and repeated success experiences, children will begin to feel that self-confidence is the more natural state.

CONFIDENCE MONTH: A CASE EXAMPLE

Confidence comes before academic success. Having a "Confidence Month," a period of time in which every child has 100 percent success, can provide the much-needed foundation for students' academic progress during the rest of the year. Trying to teach children who are vulnerable, frightened, negative, fearful of failure, insecure, and so on is like pouring water into a glass with no bottom. Confidence is the bottom in that glass.

Structuring the classroom to ensure success for every child will require changes in activities, assignments, and delivery of information. The changes in each classroom will vary according to the needs of students and resources available to the teacher. Regardless of what needs to be done, the goal is for every child to experience success to develop the foundation of confidence. Here is how one teacher changed his classroom to build students' confidence.

Mr. Perry is a fifth-grade teacher assigned to the lowest level math class. These students have all experienced failure and all have severe difficulty in math. They hate the subject, avoid it at all costs, and feel very unsure and deflated when doing math. Mr. Perry has decided that, if he attempts to build math skills on these students' inadequate foundation of confidence, he will only be repeating what they have already experienced: failure.

At this point Mr. Perry contacts parents and informs them that he will be using Positive Restructuring in his classroom. By sending home parent "news notes" like those at the end of this book, he explains the importance of confidence and tells parents he believes their children need a foundation of success in math on which he can build. He stresses that the problem is not because the students can't do the work, but that they have not been sufficiently "primed." Mr. Perry tells the parents that he needs their help for 30 days so he can build up his students' confidence. After answering parents' concerns and reassuring them that he feels Positive Restructuring will work (especially since nothing else has up to this point), he asks them for their support.

Week 1

When the children come into class on the first day, Mr. Perry informs them that, together, they are going to build their confidence in math. He reassures them that this will not happen overnight but that they will see changes by the end of the first month of school.

Then comes the hard part: Mr. Perry tells his students that, for the next 30 days, they will be taking tests. (You can imagine the responses!) He lets students voice their concerns and passes out the first test. It includes 10 kindergarten-level math problems. The students start to laugh; some joke and some get angry with Mr. Perry for asking them to do "baby work." Calmly, Mr. Perry tells the class that you have to crawl before you can walk, so the students complete the test. He scores it and returns it immediately. Needless to say, everyone gets 100. Then he hands out another test, this time with kindergarten-level subtraction problems. Again, everyone gets 100. If they need addition or subtraction tables to do the problems, Mr. Perry lets them use them. His goal is *complete* success. That class period the children take two tests: Everyone gets 100 on each test, and everyone receives praise.

For the rest of the week, Mr. Perry keeps up the kindergarten math, increasing the number of problems but never increasing the difficulty. Again he allows students to use tables, but by the end of this first week, not many students are using them. Knowing they may use the tables if they need them gives students a sense of empowerment.

By the end of the first week Mr. Perry has given 10 tests. All children have an average of 100. What begins to emerge in students is hope, another important component in building confidence. Hope begins as the students experience success and change their perceptions of themselves.

Week 2

By the second week the students are on to first-grade math and, again, every child has been successful. The lowest average is 98 percent, and the students who have missed points are now getting upset because they knew the problems but made careless mistakes. Being angry about getting a 98 is something many of these children had never experienced. Parents are now putting up their children's papers on the refrigerator, and the children are more willing to try.

By the end of the second week, the students have taken 25 tests and participated in 25 classroom activities, all of which were successful. Mr. Perry makes sure that he structures every test and activity to guarantee a sense of completion as well as success. Mr. Perry feels the length of the test is not as crucial as having the students complete it.

Week 3

By the third week the class is on to third-grade math. All the students show a marked difference in their perceptions of themselves and others. Some children are now being seen as at the top of the class, even though everyone still has averages in the 90s.

What Mr. Perry also begins to notice by the third week is that the defensive posture, negative remarks, self-criticism, despondency, and hopelessness of many children have started to wane. As confidence begins to rise, the students' need for protective defenses drops dramatically.

Week 4

By the fourth week the children are doing fourth-grade work and, although averages begin to drop somewhat, no one has lower than a 90. Most of the errors are from carelessness, not from a lack of understanding.

At the end of 30 days, the confidence exhibited by Mr. Perry's students in math is much greater than the parents, students, and even Mr. Perry could have imagined. The students enjoy coming to math class. At this point, students are not achieving because Mr. Perry is structuring assignments to ensure success but because they believe they can do it.

The year went very well in Mr. Perry's math class. Mr. Perry finished the fifth-grade curriculum, and the students' confidence helped them achieve into the next grade.

CHAPTER 3

Factors Involved in Low Self-Confidence

In order to develop confidence in all children, it is helpful to understand the reasons children may lack confidence in the first place. Children are exposed to a variety of stressors on any given day. These stressors may manifest themselves in school-related symptoms that result in dysfunction and a lack of confidence. All problems create tension. This tension must be relieved, either verbally or behaviorally. If a child is unable to communicate his feelings verbally, as is the case for many children, then that tension will exhibit itself in what we call *symptomatic behaviors*. Teachers see these behaviors every day in their classrooms in students experiencing learning difficulties.

Without understanding that an underlying problem exists, teachers may view the symptomatic behaviors as the problems. Just as treating a fever will never cure an infection, treating behavioral symptoms will never solve a child's underlying problems. Teachers need to recognize the symptom patterns of more serious conditions so they can make proper referrals. Even if correctly identified, a child's symptomatic behavior may take a while to dissipate. During this time, teachers can work toward calming the child, providing suitable boundaries, reducing classroom frustration, and preserving self-confidence.

Factors that can contribute to stress in students generally fall into the eight categories next discussed. Any of these factors can create academic, behavioral, or social problems, in turn undermining students' confidence and self-esteem.

ACADEMIC FACTORS

There will be times when academic deficits will impair a child's ability to function in the classroom. Some of the factors that can contribute to academic dysfunction are as follows:

- Developmental reading disorders
- Developmental math disorders
- Developmental writing disorders
- Poor prior teaching
- Lack of basic skills
- Inconsistency of parenting or teaching during critical periods of skill development
- Problems in concept formation
- Lack of reinforcement

Whatever the cause, academic problems need to be remedied quickly to head off additional problems. Underachievement due to academic factors in spite of adequate intelligence is frustrating to students, teachers, and parents alike. Many times, problems can be resolved with extra help, tutors, reinforcement, and so on. However, if academic problems remain unidentified for a long period of time, secondary psychological factors may begin to develop.

ENVIRONMENTAL FACTORS

Environmental factors are factors the child may be exposed to at home or in the community that affect the child's ability to function in school. These factors may include the following home issues:

- Parental abuse
- Parental conflict

- Separation and/or divorce
- Family illness
- Economic hardship
- Loss of parent's job
- Moving into a new neighborhood
- Serious sibling rivalry
- Family mental illness
- Alcoholism or drug abuse

Environmental factors may also concern community issues such as these:

- Problems with neighbors
- Poor reputation in the neighborhood
- Isolation of family from neighbors
- Problems with the law

These factors tend to add a great deal to a child's stress, which then may manifest itself in school symptoms. One needs to be aware of the possibility that classroom symptoms resulting in dysfunction may actually have their roots in issues outside of school.

INTELLECTUAL FACTORS

At times, a child's difficulties in school may be the result of intellectual factors. When these factors are present, the child's stress may emerge in a variety of symptoms. Two factors fall under this category:

- Undetected limited intellectual ability
- Undetected gifted intellectual capacity

Undetected limited intellectual ability can cause a great deal of stress in a child who fears social ridicule, teacher reaction and disappointment, negative parental reaction and disappointment, and so on. This problem may not always be detected early. Some teachers may misinterpret this factor as immaturity, stubbornness, or lack of motivation. When intellectual limits are not quickly identified, the child deals with the stress of the situation through many symptoms (e.g., avoidance, procrastination).

Undetected gifted intellectual ability can be equally as stressful. Gifted children will often be bored in class and get into trouble as a result of lack of direction and stimulation. A gifted mind needs stimulation in order to run properly. Teachers may not detect giftedness for several reasons. One is that they may be focusing on the negative symptoms manifested by the child. In their minds, giftedness and behavioral problems do not coexist. Second, teachers may feel inadequate to deal with such intellectually capable students and want to avoid possible ego-deflating situations.

In either case, intellectual factors need to be identified early. Understanding the symptom patterns that may identify these problems will help the child succeed in school and will promote the self-confidence the child needs to continue doing well.

LINGUISTIC FACTORS

Language provides the foundation upon which communication, problem solving, integration, analysis, and synthesis of knowledge take place. Therefore, deficits in language can have a profound impact on the ability of a child to learn and function competently and confidently in the world.

Difficulties in language development resulting in classroom symptoms may arise in the following areas, among others:

- Nonverbal language
- Oral language (listening and speaking)

- Written language (reading and writing)
- Pragmatic language (using language for a specific purpose, such as asking for help)
- Phonology
- Audiology
- Word retrieval
- Articulation

How quickly a person can access words or ideas in memory further influences that person's use of language. A child who must struggle to find an appropriate term is at a great disadvantage in a learning and social environment. As she grapples to retrieve a word, others have moved on. She may also miss critical pieces of knowledge, connect incorrect bits of information in memory, or have ineffective means of showing others all that she knows. Such problems can result in lowered levels of achievement, self-esteem, and self-confidence.

MEDICAL FACTORS

Medical factors that may contribute to a child's academic dysfunction and lack of self-confidence are numerous. For the most part, teachers may assume that any serious medical condition has already been identified by the child's pediatrician or parent. However, this may not always be the case, especially in the case of very young children. Some of the most common medical problems that may impair a child's ability to function adequately in the classroom and thus affect self-confidence include the following:

- Attention-Deficit/Hyperactivity Disorder (AD/HD)
- Vision problems
- Hearing problems
- Neurological problems

- Muscular problems
- Coordination problems

PERCEPTUAL FACTORS

At times perceptual difficulties can impair a child's ability to function in the classroom. Perceptual problems may slow down the processing of information, thereby interfering in the child's ability to receive, organize, memorize, or express information. Although perceptual deficits are often misunderstood or undiagnosed, they do account for a number of problems in the classroom.

Identifying symptoms that may be caused by serious perceptual deficits, then treating those deficits, can reduce a child's frustration and improve self-confidence, both in and out of the classroom.

PSYCHOLOGICAL FACTORS

Psychological factors that may contribute to a child's dysfunction in school include but are not limited to the following:

- Depression
- Anxiety
- Eating disorders
- Personality disorders
- Schizophrenia
- Phobias
- Obsessive-compulsive disorder
- Substance abuse
- Sleep disorders
- Oppositional-defiant disorder
- Conduct disorder

In addition to specific mental problems, the psychological stress of today's society may account for a large percentage of children's classroom problems. Once problems are identified, then useful treatment plans can be devised, including the home, the school psychologist or an outside therapist, medication (if necessary), and classroom management techniques. Proper treatment can reduce the secondary effects of the symptoms and help preserve children's self-esteem.

SOCIAL FACTORS

Social factors may contribute to a child's stress and consequently interfere with learning and the development of self-confidence. Although social status is an important factor at many ages, it becomes more of a factor as adolescence approaches. Sometimes a student's low energy for school is the result of his intense need for energy to cope with his social world or social conflicts. Social factors that may lower energy and result in academic dysfunction include the following:

- Peer rejection
- Preoccupation with boyfriends or girlfriends
- Low social status
- Social victimization (e.g., scapegoating, being the victim of bullying)
- Need to be in social control
- Peer competition
- Social isolation
- Social overindulgence

When children have serious social concerns, their symptoms can be intense. If not identified early, they can lead to numerous secondary issues, including a breakdown of self-confidence.

CHAPTER 4

Recognizing Students With Low Self-Confidence

Classroom teachers are usually the first to identify children who lack confidence and are at risk for school failure. However, without knowing what behaviors actually represent deeper problems, teachers may not notice or may misinterpret them.

One goal of Positive Restructuring is to learn ways to identify students whose self-confidence has been compromised. As explained in chapter 1, children who lack confidence may exhibit low frustration tolerance, blame others for their problems, or lose perspective easily. These and other behavioral symptoms—the result of unresolved conflicts or problems—are the signals that allow us to realize that difficulties exist.

SIGNS OF LOW SELF-CONFIDENCE

A student lacking in confidence is usually a student who has experienced emotional, social, environmental, or academic stress and/or failure. As a result of internal turmoil, the student generates symptoms in a dynamic attempt to alleviate anxiety. These symptoms can show up in the form of many different behavior patterns. Some of the more common ones include the following:

- Adequate or high first-quarter grades followed by a downward trend, leading to failure in the final quarter
- Excessive absences or tardiness

- High achievement scores and high school-abilities indexes with a history of low academic performance

- Consistent failure in at least two subjects in two or more quarters

- A history of parent "coverage" for inappropriate behavior, poor work performance, poor attitude, failures, or absences

- Wandering school halls after hours with no direction or purpose

- Blaming others for poor academic or behavioral performance

- Recent stressful experiences (e.g., family separation or divorce, death of a parent, parent's loss of employment)

- Frequent visits to the school nurse

- Social withdrawal from peers, with attention turning toward relationships with adults

In younger children, lack of confidence sometimes shows up as difficulty separating from the parent at the start of the school day. Although separation anxiety is normal in children ages 7 and younger, it can be a sign of serious problems after that. Other behavior patterns can signal low confidence as well.

AVOIDANCE BEHAVIORS

Avoidance behaviors in students are a particularly telling sign—usually an early one—of learning problems. Students use these techniques to avoid what they perceive as potential failures or ego-deflating situations. Specifically, they are attempting to avoid these eventualities:

- Showing their parents or teachers that they are incompetent

- Dealing with anger and frustration from parents or teachers

- Coming face to face with their own inadequacy
- Dealing with peer pressure and ridicule

In the classroom, avoidance behaviors can take any of the forms next described.

Selective Forgetting

If a child knows the batting averages of all baseball players, the words from most songs on the radio, and the times of most TV shows but habitually "forgets" to bring home his math book, the child may be exhibiting selective forgetting. The forgetfulness usually centers on areas of learning that the child finds frustrating.

Forgetting to Write Down Assignments

All students forget to write down assignments from time to time. If this symptom continues even after repeated requests (or threats), the child is most likely trying to avoid a potential failure experience.

Taking Hours to Complete Homework

In this avoidance pattern the child labors over homework for a time far longer than necessary. Delaying completion means delaying failure. This symptom also occurs if a child is under tension and having difficulty concentrating for long periods of time. In this case, she will tend to "burn out" quickly, then daydream the time away.

Finishing Class Work or Homework Very Quickly

The child exhibiting this symptom is trying to get the ego-threatening situation (the class work or homework) over with as quickly as possible. The student rushes through assignments with little if any care or patience. Getting the work over as quickly as possible makes it seem to the student as if it never existed.

Not Being Able to Get Started With Homework

When a child's anxiety level is high it is very difficult for the child to "start the engine." He may spend a great deal of time getting ready for homework by arranging books, sharpening pencils, getting paper out, opening textbooks, getting a glass of water, going to the bathroom, and so on. Once again, the child is trying to avoid the task that he finds threatening.

Bringing Home Unfinished Class Work

A child can exhibit this symptom for several reasons. One reason could be that the child has a low energy level and therefore has difficulty dealing with tasks involving sustained concentration. A second reason could be that the child is dependent upon parental assistance with homework. If the child's parent constantly sits next to the child when she does homework, the child may come to feel helpless without the parent. A third reason concerns the child's need for attention. Bringing home unfinished class work extends the attention the child receives from the parent; however, these situations usually become more tense and negative as the hours progress and the parent's patience waivers.

Leaving Long-Term Assignments Until the Last Minute

Consistent avoidance of school-related tasks, especially long-term ones, is frequently a symptom of low energy. The behavior is analogous to avoiding paying a big bill when one has very little money. Another way to avoid paying a bill is to forget the bill exists. Similarly, children who are anxious about being able to complete an assignment try to wish the assignment out of existence and on some level believe that it will magically be finished without any participation on their part.

Complaining of Headaches, Stomachaches, or Other Pains

High tension levels over an extended period of time may result in a child's somatic (bodily) complaints. These complaints,

while real to the child, may indicate his avoidance of an uncomfortable or potentially ego-deflating situation. The physical discomfort or ailment becomes the excuse for not performing well or not performing at all.

Engaging in Spotlight Behaviors

"Spotlight behaviors" are behaviors that focus attention on the child—calling out, laughing loudly, getting up out of seat, annoying other children. Some children use such behaviors to alleviate tension and may even hope to get into trouble and be sent out of the room. In this way they will not have to deal with possible academic failure. Spotlight behaviors can also reflect a child's need for control. However, the more controlling a child is, the more out of control that child may feel. Yet another reason is to gain the teacher's attention. In this way, the child is determining when she gets attention, not the teacher. If this is the case, it is best for the teacher to pay attention to the child when the child is not exhibiting the problem behavior.

SEVERITY OF PROBLEMS

As we have said, symptomatic behaviors that indicate low self-confidence may include everything from failure to complete homework to fear of new situations, from impulsivity to argumentativeness. These symptoms may or may not indicate a serious problem. The following guidelines are helpful in determining the severity of the situation.

Frequency

Consider how often the symptoms occur. The greater the frequency, the greater the chance of a serious problem.

Duration

Consider how long the symptoms last. The longer the duration, the more serious the problem.

Intensity

Consider how serious the symptoms are at the time of occurrence. The more intense the symptoms, the more serious the problem.

Symptoms that are ways to relieve tension usually indicate conflicts and fears within the child. All conflicts require energy, and the greater the number or more serious the conflict, the greater expense of energy required. Everyone has only a certain amount of available energy, so the energy required to deal with conflicts tends to be drained away from other processes, such as memory, attention, impulse control, and so forth. These are the areas in which children most commonly express symptoms, either in the classroom or at home.

When a child is troubled by serious conflicts, available energy must be diverted to deal with the conflicts, like white blood cells drawn to an infection, and the child has less energy available to keep things in perspective.

SIGNS OF SELF-CONFIDENCE

At school, the self-confident child exhibits such behaviors as good concentration, responsibility for schoolwork, consistency, age-appropriate attention span, flexibility, appropriate memory, high frustration tolerance, appropriate peer interactions, adequate organization, and an appropriate ability to focus on tasks. Parents notice these behaviors at home when the child does homework, and educators notice them at school. Not every self-confident, conflict-free child exhibits these behaviors all the time, but the child's habits and behaviors are predominately positive and constructive.

Positive behavior patterns at home include normal striving for parental approval, willingness to reason and to try, appropriate judgment, and age-appropriate responses to discipline. A relatively conflict-free child will usually have little difficulty falling asleep. Although the child may have occasional problems waking up, as many of us do, they will not interfere with her ability to get to school. Socially, the child will generally maintain interactions, show a willingness to try new social experiences, and treat her peers appropriately. These patterns may vary to some degree and still be within normal limits.

REFERRING STUDENTS FOR HELP

Once a student has been identified as having low self-confidence, it is important for teachers and parents to understand how this may interfere with the child's ability to learn. Children who lack confidence are not "stubborn" or "lazy." The real reasons for a lack of academic production or inappropriate behavior may concern the dynamic state of low self-confidence. Teachers or parents who suspect that a child is experiencing difficulty because he exhibits a negative symptomatic pattern should schedule a consultation with the school psychologist or, in some cases, a therapist in the community.

It is important to remember that such symptoms only occur as a result of a deeper undefined problem. Once the problem is identified and resolved, and once the tension is alleviated, the negative symptomatic behavior will dissipate. If caught early, many such problems can be resolved in a relatively brief period of time.

If the underlying problem is not identified for months or years, the treatment period will be longer. As the child begins to verbalize the issues and find better ways of coping, the tension diminishes. As the tension is reduced, the child's need for symptomatic behavior also diminishes, and confidence-building opportunities increase.

CHAPTER 5

Positive and Negative Teacher Characteristics

More and more, teachers are becoming a primary influence in children's lives, and in some cases they may be the only healthy adults some children encounter during the day. Twenty-five years ago, family structures were very different, and teachers did not require the depth and variety of social/emotional skills that are required of today's teachers. Teachers today are not only educators, but therapists, parent substitutes, mentors, advocates, and more.

It stands to reason that a teacher's personality and teaching style can have a profound impact on children's academic performance and general development. In chapter 1, we gave some examples of positive and negative teaching. In this chapter, we urge you to consider how aspects of your personality are expressed in your teaching style and how they affect children in your classroom. So let's consider teacher characteristics that facilitate or inhibit the growth of self-confidence.

No single aspect of a teacher's personality is responsible for improving or destroying a student's self-confidence. For example, a very strict teacher who is kind, fair, genuine, logical, and nurturing may facilitate the growth of self-confidence despite being very strict. On the other hand, a teacher who is funny but unstructured and disorganized may not facilitate chidren's self-confidence. Despite the fact that the children love this teacher, they may not gain confidence if the teacher cannot provide the real-life success experiences necessary for its growth.

POSITIVE CHARACTERISTICS

What personal characteristics in teachers facilitate the growth of self-confidence in students? The following aspects of teacher personality most commonly increase the chances that children will develop positive self-images in the classroom.

Genuineness

This quality is exhibited by teachers who . . .

- Create a student-centered classroom environment
- Go beyond what is expected of them to promote students' well-being
- Are easily approachable
- Are honest and up-front with students
- Follow through on what they say
- Are consistent in their methods
- Are not fake or hypocritical

Fairness

Teachers with this quality . . .

- Can admit to making a mistake
- Give assignments that take into account students' needs and levels of ability
- Give assignments reasonable in length, with the main goal of successful completion
- Give tests that stick to what has been taught
- Take a commonsense approach to grading homework and essays
- Give helpful comments for improvement
- Give students advance notice of quizzes and tests
- Do not seek to "get" children by giving difficult assignments or tests

Organization

Teachers who have this characteristic . . .

- Maintain order and routine in their classrooms
- Provide students with structure and logical rules that apply to all
- Teach students to organize their materials, desks, and lockers
- Have well-planned lessons with logical presentation and relevant follow-up assignments
- Hand back tests and essays in a reasonable amount of time

Logic and Common Sense

This quality is expressed by teachers who . . .

- Recognize that students have good and bad days
- Understand that forces outside of the classroom may be affecting a student's performance
- Know that the classroom is not the center of the universe

Ability to Set Clear Boundaries

Teachers with this ability will . . .

- Take a stand to promote fairness and enforce classroom rules, even if it makes them unpopular
- Set clear and fair boundaries for students who may be out of control
- Run the classroom with a sense of conviction rather than by fear or intimidation

Sense of Humor or Lightheartedness

This quality is exhibited by teachers who . . .

- Place a priority on important issues and understand that to err is human
- Allow students to explore their "child" side without admonishing them to grow up

- Are able to laugh at themselves when they make a mistake
- Understand the difference between telling jokes and making fun of or belittling students

Ability to Give Compliments

Teachers with this characteristic can . . .

- Spontaneously compliment students for their achievements and for trying their best
- Find positive things to tell students before making suggestions on how to improve
- Make constructive comments on tests and essays without devaluing students' efforts
- Provide students with small notes and cards recognizing a good job, a commonsense decision, assistance to another student, and so forth

Ability to Admit Mistakes

Teachers who possess this quality will . . .

- Admit their own mistakes to let students see that mistakes present a learning opportunity.
- Not be afraid to show students how to correct a decision that is obviously wrong

Willingness to Listen

Teachers who can listen . . .

- Put aside time to sit down with students who need to say something
- Understand that reaching out to an adult is a difficult step for many students, especially for those who have no one to listen to them at home
- Teach students that being listened to does not always mean that someone will agree or be able to do what they ask

Approachability

Teachers with this quality . . .

- Have the ability to make students feel at ease when they come to ask questions
- Exhibit a sense of warmth and comfort
- Cultivate an atmosphere in which children do not fear negative reactions

NEGATIVE CHARACTERISTICS

Now let's take a look at some personality characteristics that increase the chances of children's developing negative self-images in the classroom.

Ego Teaching

Teachers with this characteristic usually . . .

- Have unrealistically high standards that create stress
- Give long homework assignments designed to show parents how good a job they are doing
- Give difficult tests that require children to learn minutiae
- Have grading systems that create numerous failures
- Command respect by frightening and intimidating students

Excessive Criticism

This characteristic is exhibited by teachers who . . .

- Criticize children in public
- Criticize more often than they compliment
- Believe that compliments and rewards reduce their authority
- Use sarcasm as a means of motivation
- Are quick to blame a child's lack of progress or poor grades on the student rather than analyzing the situation for possible teaching problems

Unreasonability

This characteristic is exhibited when teachers . . .

- Refuse to listen to children
- Make demands without giving reasons
- Provide work and experiences that are too difficult for children to finish without parental help
- Are never willing to hear students' explanations for not meeting requirements

Narcissism

This aspect of personality is reflected when teachers . . .

- Use children to keep the spotlight on themselves
- Give a great deal of work but rarely hand it back or hand it back with few or no comments
- Focus attention on themselves rather than the needs of students
- Take it out on students if they have a bad day

Rigidity

This quality is expressed by teachers who . . .

- Take everything seriously
- Are unwilling to change their minds
- Are unwilling to admit mistakes
- Will stick with something even if it makes little sense or has little educational value

Punishment Orientation

Teachers with this mentality . . .

- Punish students for relatively small infractions
- Make a public spectacle of students

- Hold students' behavior or performance up to their peers for ridicule
- Refuse to allow students to explain their side of a situation
- Always see students' explanations as excuses or attempts to control the situation
- Enforce rules with harsh, unrealistic consequences

Disorganization

Teachers with this quality tend to . . .

- Change the rules frequently, thus creating confusion in students
- Give tests or quizzes without letting students know in advance
- Lose students' work
- Appear to be "winging it," with no real plan or structure

Unpredictability

Teachers with this quality will . . .

- Change rules without informing students, sometimes until they break them
- Have different rules for different people
- Be nice to a student one day and not another, for no apparent reason

Lack of Control

Teachers who exhibit this quality . . .

- Have no set classroom rules for discipline or opportunities for reward
- Always seem to be yelling and screaming
- Make extreme threats that rarely are enforced
- Let the students "run the show"

Create Anxiety in Students

Teachers who do this . . .

- Say things to scare children (for instance, "You'll be lucky if you get a 65 on tomorrow's test.")
- Never offer reassurance before or after tests
- Inform students of how much trouble they will be in if they don't do well on this test or assignment
- Create self-doubt in students

"Gotcha" Mentality

Teachers who have this characteristic . . .

- Hope to catch students making mistakes
- Always correct students for breaking rules, no matter how minor
- Will seize any opportunity to exhibit power over students
- Will publicly broadcast what they uncover about students' infractions

Overreactivity

Teachers who exhibit this quality will . . .

- Turn minor events into major crises
- Enforce punishments inappropriate to the situation
- Scream and yell at students for minor infractions

Although successful experiences are the most critical factor in building confidence, a positive teacher with a constructive teaching style can go a long way toward breaking down initial resistance barriers. Positive or negative, a teacher's personality and teaching style directly affect students' sense of self—sometimes even into adulthood.

CHAPTER 6

Classroom Practices for Building Confidence

Confident children seem to share certain characteristics. In their relationships with both teachers and parents, they show in many ways that they are empowered, hopeful, autonomous, resilient, and secure. They are also accomplished, receive recognition for their accomplishments, and persevere even when things don't go as they would like. Finally, they genuinely seem to enjoy life, both at school and at home. The ideas described here, if practiced in the classroom, will help students enjoy the environment they are in and believe in themselves as they never have before. The key lies in being open and creative to these ideas.

EMPOWERMENT

Empowerment means being given the authority or power to act as you wish. For many students, knowing they are empowered is actually more important than actually exercising that power. In the classroom, the empowerment that comes from having educational tools they can turn to promotes a sense of security and helps build the foundation of confidence. Without a sense of empowerment, students may become rigid and hesitant, always waiting for you to tell them what to do next or how to solve problems.

Classroom Practices

- Allowing the use of . . .

    Math tables and formulas during tests

    Calculators to check work

    Computer resources to find answers

    Dictionaries for in-class writing assignments

- Giving examples similar to upcoming problems or questions

- Permitting students to collaborate with one another to find answers

HOPE

Hope is desire accompanied by the expectation of fulfillment, the genuine belief that things will work out as we wish. When students feel hopeless, they feel powerless. If they have hope and believe they can succeed, students will tend to take more risks and chances.

Classroom Practices

- Providing shorter but more frequent assignments

- Checking small groups of problems at a time so students can correct errors before they have finished an entire assignment

- Letting students know that if they fulfill certain requirements, they can expect to get good grades

- Letting students know specifically what is required to earn a certain grade

- Providing students with short, positive daily progress reports

- Sending parents weekly notes on positive aspects of the students' progress

Ya eyyühellezîne âmenû
zkürullâhe zikran kesîra

"Ey iman edenler, Allah'ı
çok anın, çok yâd edin.

100 defa
Sübhanallâhi ve bihamdihî
Sübhanallâhil azîm

AUTONOMY

Another important quality children with confidence have is autonomy, or the belief that you have the ability to govern yourself. According to James Raffini, "This need for self-determination is satisfied when individuals are free to behave of their own volition—to engage in activities because they want to, not because they have to. At its core is the freedom to choose and to have choices, rather than being forced or coerced to behave according to the desires of another."*

Classroom Practices

- Giving students time to do independent work, enjoy hobbies, or pursue areas of interest
- Allowing students time to work on their own ideas
- Giving students choices or options for projects rather than telling them what must be done
- Allowing students to share their own original ideas with others
- Giving students responsibility for aspects of their own learning (e.g., determining the order of lessons, types of evaluation, timelines for completion)

RESILIENCY

Resiliency is the ability to bounce back from unsuccessful experiences. A student with high resiliency who fails a test is likely to be willing to look at the factors that contributed to his failure, then try again. A student who has low resiliency is more inclined to give up on all future tests. Resiliency is an important component of self-confidence and success. Without resiliency, students may resist or give up on schoolwork entirely.

---

*From *150 Ways to Increase Intrinsic Motivation in the Classroom* by J. Raffini, 1996, New York: Simon and Schuster.

Classroom Practices

- Providing repeated successful experiences

- Providing students with the opportunity to correct their work to master concepts and improve their grades

- Giving students the opportunity to drop their lowest grade in each subject so one bad score does not destroy their motivation

SECURITY

A classroom is a child's second home. As a teacher, it is your responsibility to create a warm and comforting environment so the children in your classroom can work to their potential without worry.

Classroom Practices

- Providing predictability by outlining the day's activities (or week's, or term's)

- Following through on what you say you will do; not making promises you cannot keep

- Providing opportunities throughout the day for students to approach you with questions, comments, or concerns

ACCOMPLISHMENT

A feeling of accomplishment is the sense that you have brought something about by your own efforts. Confidence is the belief that one's behavior will, for the most part, lead to the successful completion of tasks or projects. In Positive Restructuring this sense of accomplishment is enhanced by assigning work that will ensure students' success.

Feeling a sense of accomplishment does not mean that a task or assignment must be completed in its entirety. A child can feel good about herself because she was able to find a specific answer to part of an assignment, persevered in her work, or gave her best effort.

Classroom Practices

- Giving shorter but more frequent assignments
- Supporting parents in checking homework every night
- Providing parents with a list of homework assignments so that they can follow up at home
- Giving students checklists of work they have completed
- Providing sufficient time for students to complete assignments (or extra time for students who need it)
- Using Success Bank Accounts (see chapter 7)

RECOGNITION

Everyone needs to be recognized—to receive special notice or attention. Parents normally provide much of a child's recognition. However, teachers are a close second to parents when it comes to a child's desire to please and be recognized for performance and effort. Without recognition, students may lose the desire to try, believing that no one cares what they do. Recognition enhances motivation, especially intrinsic motivation—that is, choosing to do an activity not for external rewards but for the internal satisfaction derived from the activity itself. Although recognition is an extrinsic, or external, reward, over time it becomes internalized. Recognition also reduces students' need to bribe, threaten, negotiate, and demand.

Classroom Practices

- Providing frequent written or verbal validation (e.g., "Good effort," "Thanks for helping Billy yesterday," etc.)
- Giving spontaneous notes of praise

- Writing positive letters or notes to parents
- Depending on grade level, awarding stickers, gold stars, and the like
- Complimenting students anytime they behave positively (in other words, "catching them being good")

PERSEVERANCE

Perseverance means to pursue a goal in the face of difficulty, discouragement, or opposition. Continuing when the going is rough means that students have built enough confidence to have internalized the belief that there is a direct relationship between effort and achievement. Once students have internalized this belief, they are less frustrated and more resilient, solution oriented, willing to take chances, and goal directed.

Classroom Practices

- Giving rewards for striving to succeed
- Complimenting students for working hard (e.g., recognizing the sustained effort a student is making on a math problem)
- Breaking down long-term assignments into manageable steps, and rewarding students for achieving each step
- Working alongside students to help them complete assignments

ENJOYMENT

Sadly, when asked what they think of school, many children respond in a negative manner. Too often, enjoyment has had a bad reputation in schools. Many educators believe that learning is supposed to be hard work, and, if the work is enjoyable, it cannot be serious or significant. Parents and teachers need to change this belief. Just because students enjoy the learning

process doesn't mean the classroom is too lax, easy, or unstructured. On the contrary, if children are happy, not stressed out,
their motivation for learning is enhanced.

Classroom Practices

- Providing fun activities at the end of each day
- Starting each day with a light, funny, or exciting activity
- Having students bring in and share activities and games
  from home
- Having students share hobbies on certain days

CHAPTER 7

Success Bank Accounts

Success Bank Accounts are a way to give students a series of realistic, successful experiences that strengthen the foundation of confidence. Success Bank Accounts can be developed in any or all of the following areas:

- Math Success Bank Account
- Spelling Success Bank Account
- Writing Success Bank Account
- Reading Success Bank Account
- Social Studies Success Bank Account
- Science Success Bank Account
- Social Success Bank Account
- Creative Success Bank Account (music, art, drama, and so on)
- Jobs and Responsibilities Success Bank Account
- Recreational Success Bank Account (sports, hobbies, and the like)
- Home Experiences Success Bank Account

Each student starts a folder, with each account kept on a separate Success Bank Account sheet. (See the sample sheet, for math success, on the next page.) Whenever the student experiences success, the student writes the date and type of success

MATH SUCCESS BANK ACCOUNT

Student _____ Anna _____

Date	**Type of success**
2/3	Completed homework.
2/4	Got 8 out of 10 on quiz.
2/5	Paid attention during math lesson.
2/6	Started difficult math project.
2/7	Got a 90 percent on math test after rechecking.

on the appropriate sheet. (You can prompt the student to jot down the experience or write it for the child if necessary.)

Success Bank Accounts are not meant to be time consuming. You can copy the blank form on page 61 as you need. A few entries a day on these forms are sufficient. Remember, every successful experience is one more brick in the foundation of success. If you choose, you might want students to decorate their Success Bank Account folders. After they do this task, it can become the first entry in their Creative Success Bank Account.

At the end of 4 weeks, the Success Bank Account sheets should include at least 35 to 50 successful experiences in each area. Having this written record will enable students to see and feel success; if students doubt their abilities, you can show them their bank accounts of successes to help reshape their thinking. Students' successes grow like a real bank account, and their experiences offer them a real basis for self-confidence.

Here are some entries we have seen students make in areas other than math.

Spelling Success

- Studied for the test.
- Corrected misspelled words.
- Learned "i" before "e" rule.
- Entered spelling bee.

Writing Success

- I wrote a great essay today.
- Started to write a short story.
- My handwriting is improving.
- I was able to write two paragraphs today without help.

Reading Success

- I read two books this week.
- I read an article from the newspaper last night.
- I read three comic books at home from cover to cover.
- My parents took me to the bookstore, and I bought two great books to read on vacation.
- I read a whole page without making a mistake.
- I was able to read in front of my reading group today.

Social Studies Success

- I finished my part of the group project.
- I got a good grade on the social studies quiz.
- I studied last night for an hour for my test.
- I read the social studies chapter to my parents.

Science Success

- My parents bought me a chemistry set.
- I did a science experiment with my dad yesterday.
- I finished my science lab early.
- I understood the science homework without having to ask for help.
- I covered my science book with a neat cover I picked out myself.

Social Success

- Asked Billy over after school.
- Spoke with Tara today.
- Played with Robert at recess.
- Sat with John at lunch.
- Asked two boys to my party.

Creative Success

- I started piano lessons today.
- I have now been taking guitar lessons for 1 year.
- I tried out for the play.
- I signed up for dance lessons after school today.
- Today the art teacher said she loved my project.

Jobs and Responsibilities Success

- Today I cleaned out my desk and organized my locker.
- Today was my day to collect the milk money, and I did it without having to be told.
- This morning I sharpened all the pencils.
- Last night I got all my things ready for school so I would not have to rush this morning.

Recreational Success

- Today I started a baseball card collection.
- Today I walked with my mom.
- Yesterday after school, I jogged 1 mile.
- I signed up for the girls' soccer team.
- I started collecting coins.
- I am now able to walk to school every day.

Home Experiences Success

- Yesterday my mom and I baked a cake.
- Last night I helped my sister do her homework.
- Today we are going to the wallpaper store, and I am going to pick out new paper for my room.
- Last night I washed the dishes without being told.
- I got 2 dollars allowance for doing my jobs and put the money in my piggy bank.

Parent News Notes include a special Success Bank Account sheet for at-home use, along with suggestions for using it. The combination of parent and teacher confidence building through this technique can be very powerful.

Both teachers and parents will want to help children integrate their confidence experiences by giving lots of praise. For example, a math teacher might say to a student who completed a long homework assignment, "Wow. You must feel very proud finishing all that homework. Nice job." To a child who has successfully negotiated a compromise with a sibling, a parent might say, "I really like it when you two take turns. Good effort!"

SUCCESS BANK ACCOUNT

Student _____

Date   **Type of success**

_____   _____

_____   _____

_____   _____

_____   _____

_____   _____

_____   _____

_____   _____

_____   _____

_____   _____

_____   _____

_____   _____

_____   _____

_____   _____

CHAPTER 8

Creating Confident Children: Principles for Teachers and Parents

The following principles of Positive Restructuring are offered to help teachers and parents enhance children's positive feelings about themselves. Applying these principles will require consistency, genuineness, and discrimination on the part of teachers and parents. However, the benefits of truly integrating changes based on these principles are great. No suggestion by itself will have long-lasting effects; a combination of techniques will have greater impact.

Teachers and parents should always keep in mind that many factors not within their control (e.g., peer group, school success or failure, perceptions) will also affect children's self-esteem. However, the role of teachers and parents is a crucial one, and, by adhering to the following principles, teachers and parents can help offset children's difficulties in other areas.

Become introspective about your own issues and how they affect your teaching or parenting style.

Children need to work toward understanding their feelings about their self-worth. It is important for teachers and parents to evaluate their own feelings of self-esteem as well. If they are experiencing feelings of inadequacy, changing children's feelings about themselves will be more difficult. Improving children's self-confidence is a process that needs to be viewed in a positive way. The more teachers and parents can work to resolve their own issues, the better they will be able to help children with theirs.

Be solution oriented.

An important step in building children's self-esteem is to teach solutions rather than assign blame. Some families (and some classrooms) are very "blame oriented." When something goes wrong, family members are quick to point the finger at one another. Children who grow up in this type of environment not only become easily frustrated, they may never learn how to overcome obstacles. Teaching children solutions begins with simple statements like "Who's at fault is not important. The more important question is, What can we do so that it doesn't happen again?" A problem-solving orientation gives children a sense of control and helps promote resiliency when they are confronted with situations that could be ego deflating.

Preserve children's right to make decisions.

Despite what some children would like, families and classrooms are not democracies. However, giving children the right to make decisions that affect their daily life can only enhance their self-esteem. At home, decisions about clothing, room arrangement, friends to invite to a party, menu for dinner, and so forth give children a sense of autonomy—self-control over what happens to them. In the classroom, students might decorate classroom bulletin boards, choose activities for free time, or decide whether to have a pizza or popcorn party. Coupling a solution orientation with decision-making power can turn children's problems into positive learning experiences.

Offer alternative ways of handling a problem situation.

Some people know only one or two alternatives in handling a problem situation. After these fail, they become frustrated.

Teaching children to seek many alternative ways of handling problems or overcoming obstacles can also enhance their self-esteem. Asking children what they have tried and guiding them toward other possible solutions enlarges their problem-solving "tool box." Children with limited tools tend to avoid or flee from difficulties. The more tools children have at their disposal, the easier their lives become.

Teach children the proper labels for their feelings.

The ability to identify one's feelings is a factor in self-confidence. Children may have difficulty communicating because they lack the proper labels for their feelings. When children are unable to label a feeling, it becomes trapped, and their frustration may manifest itself in behavioral problems, physical symptoms, and the like. Parents and teachers sometimes misunderstand or misinterpret such feelings when they are manifested behaviorally. Offering children correct labels gets to the real issue. For example, you may want to say, "The feeling you are expressing sounds like anger, but it is really frustration. Frustration is feeling upset that you can't do something or get something right. Now that you know this, is there anything that is causing you frustration?" Building an emotional vocabulary allows communication and helps children deal with troubling situations.

Allow children the opportunity to repeat successful experiences.

Whenever possible, allow children the chance to handle any job or responsibility in which they have been successful. A foundation of positive experiences is necessary to build confidence, and prior success ensures that children have mastered the skills to do the job. Cooking dinner, cutting the lawn, fixing something around the house, and making a shopping list are examples of at-home jobs that can be repeated. In the classroom, erasing the chalkboard, collecting milk money, bringing notes to the office, and taking attendance can serve the same purpose.

Allow avenues for disagreement.

Children with high self-confidence feel they have a way to communicate their dissatisfaction. Even though the result may not be in their favor, the knowledge that a situation or disagreement can be discussed allows children to feel involved in their destiny. Children with low self-confidence tend to believe no one will listen if they express disagreement.

Help children set realistic goals.

Realistic goals are crucial in building confidence. Some children will set unrealistic goals, fall short, and feel like failures. If failures are repeated over a period of time, children may begin to feel a sense of urgency, leading to more unrealistic goals. This circular behavior sometimes results in children's unwillingness to venture out or take chances. The more limited children become in their experiences, the less likely their chance for success. Avoidance, passivity, and rejection of alternative ideas or experiences will only reinforce feelings of inadequacy.

Help children define their objectives.

You may want to ask children what they want to accomplish. After this, try to help them define the steps necessary to accomplish the task. Each step becomes a goal in itself. Children may be overwhelmed by a final goal but be able to handle a series of smaller steps leading to that final goal. At every step, they have the opportunity to feel accomplishment.

Use a reward system to shape positive behavior.

Punishment tells a child what not to do, whereas rewards tell them what to do. Rewarding positive behavior builds confidence. Children enjoy winning the approval of parents and teachers, especially when it comes to jobs or tasks. At-home rewards can be special trips, special time with one parent, extra time before bed, a hug and a kiss, or a note indicating appreciation for a child's effort or achievement. Monetary rewards can also be used from time to time. It can be very helpful if teachers give extra free time, tokens to be spent at the school store, or bonus points toward classroom privileges.

Don't pave all the child's roads.

Some parents and teachers make the mistake of reducing frustration for children to the point where they receive a distorted view of the world. Children with high self-esteem get frustrated. However, they tend to be more resilient because they have previously handled frustrating situations and worked out the solutions themselves. When parents rush to the aid of their children, or change the environment to prevent them from becoming frustrated, they are unwittingly reinforcing children's low self-esteem. After a while, children become dependent upon their parents to "bail them out" when they are confronted with frustration. In the classroom, teachers can let their students solve their own problems, ask them for options, and give them more time to come up with answers. To become self-confident, children need to master the environment and work toward their own solutions to challenges. The old saying "Catch me a fish and I'll eat today; teach me to fish and I'll eat forever" seems to apply.

Parent News Notes

The following Parent News Notes describe the procedures for confidence building outlined in this book. As their titles suggest, the notes introduce the idea of Confidence Month, describe Success Bank Accounts, enumerate the principles of Positive Restructuring, and give parents a number of helpful suggestions for interacting with their children.

Parent involvement is a key factor in the success of Confidence Month, as well as in continued success throughout the year. We have found that sending home two News Notes per week keeps busy parents abreast of what is happening in the classroom without overburdening them with too much reading. You can photocopy the notes as they are printed here to send home with students, or you may wish to reproduce the information in a larger format or tailor the content for your particular group. Whatever you choose, we suggest sending this information home in the following order:

1. Welcome to Confidence Month

2. Success Bank Accounts

3. Success at Home

4. Principles of Positive Restructuring

5. Guidelines for Parents (Number 1)

6. Guidelines for Parents (Number 2)

7. Guidelines for Parents (Number 3)

8. Characteristics of Confidence

WELCOME TO CONFIDENCE MONTH

All children need confidence in order to learn. Although many children are eager to learn and believe in their ability to achieve, not every child has the confidence to do well in school. In fact, trying to teach a child without confidence is like trying to build a house on sand!

Repeated Success

Confidence is the result of repeated successful experiences. If we think back to our confidence level the first time we rode a bicycle versus the 50th time, we see that what we needed to feel confident was riding the bicycle successfully, again and again. Our successes increased our confidence. Children are no different. Without repeated successful experiences, no amount of praise will help children gain the confidence they need in order to learn.

Positive Restructuring

For the next month, we will be using Positive Restructuring in our classroom. Positive Restructuring is a developmentally appropriate and organized approach to providing successful learning experiences. These first 4 weeks of school are therefore "Confidence Month." During this time, lessons will be organized so that *every child experiences success.* Success early on will provide a strong foundation for students' academic progress during the rest of the year.

How You Can Help

You can help your child build the confidence to learn by asking your child about school and celebrating his or her successes, and by recognizing your child's successes at home. Success at home might be as simple as taking out the garbage without being asked or as complicated as working out a compromise with a brother or sister who doesn't want to watch the same television program your other child does. Stay positive and give lots of support for your child's honest achievements.

As we move through these first few weeks, you'll receive additional News Notes and more suggestions for helping your child build confidence.

SUCCESS BANK ACCOUNTS

In our classroom, one way students experience success is through Success Bank Accounts. Students record their successful experiences on Success Bank Account sheets and can see for themselves that they are good learners. Their repeated successes strengthen the foundation of self-confidence.

Types of Accounts

Students keep accounts in any or all of the following areas:

- Math Success Bank Account
- Spelling Success Bank Account
- Writing Success Bank Account
- Reading Success Bank Account
- Social Studies Success Bank Account
- Science Success Bank Account
- Social Success Bank Account
- Creative Success Bank Account (music, art, drama, and so on)
- Jobs and Responsibilities Success Bank Account
- Recreational Success Bank Account (sports, hobbies, and the like)

Success Bank Account Sheets

Your child has a special folder of Success Bank Account sheets at school, with one sheet for each area chosen. Whenever your child experiences success in that area, he or she writes down the date and type of success on the appropriate sheet. Here are some examples of successes your child might record.

Writing

- I wrote a great essay today.
- My handwriting is improving.
- I was able to write two paragraphs today without help.

Reading

- I read two books this week.
- I read a whole page without making a mistake.
- I was able to read in front of my reading group today.

Science

- I did a science experiment with my dad yesterday.
- I finished my science lab early.
- I understood the science homework without having to ask for help.

Jobs and responsibilities

- I cleaned out my desk and organized my locker.
- I collected the milk money and took it to the office without having to be told.
- I remembered to bring my tennis shoes for gym class.

Recreation

- Today I started a baseball card collection.
- Yesterday after school, I jogged 1 mile.
- I signed up for the soccer team.

The next News Note will explain how you can keep a Success Bank Account sheet at home.

SUCCESS AT HOME

If you wish, you can encourage your child to keep a Success Bank Account at home, using the sheet that accompanies this News Note. If you do, here are some entries your child might make:

- Yesterday Mom and I baked a cake.
- I helped my sister do her homework.
- Last night I washed the dishes without being told.
- I practiced the piano today for 30 minutes.
- Dad said I was really growing up.

Even if you don't use an at-home Success Bank Account, "catching your child being good" can help your child build confidence. Here are just a few examples of things you might say when you see your child doing something positive:

- Your child gets up and dressed on time: You say, "Good morning! Your outfit sure looks nice today."
- Your child has been playing well with a brother or sister: You say, "I really like it when you two take turns. Good effort!"
- Your child cleans up his or her room: You say, "Boy, it looks beautiful in here. I'm very proud of you."

When your child does something positive, recognize it and encourage him or her to record it on the Success Bank Account sheet if you are using one. Every family's situation is different, and you may feel more comfortable using different words to show your child you notice and appreciate his or her efforts. It doesn't really matter what words you use: Your child will know what you mean.

HOME EXPERIENCES SUCCESS BANK ACCOUNT

Date   **Type of success**

_____   _____

_____   _____

_____   _____

_____   _____

_____   _____

_____   _____

_____   _____

_____   _____

_____   _____

_____   _____

_____   _____

_____   _____

_____   _____

_____   _____

_____   _____

PRINCIPLES OF POSITIVE RESTRUCTURING

Now that you know about Confidence Month and have seen how Success Bank Accounts work, you might be interested in knowing some of the principles of Positive Restructuring and why systematically providing students with successful learning experiences helps them gain confidence.

Principle 1: Every child is capable of being successful.

Students need to believe from the start that they are capable of success in some or all areas of school. What prevents many students from embracing this belief is the amount, type, and level of work presented to them, coupled with a definition of success based on group comparison (for example, tests, grade-level standards, etc.). When group comparison is the benchmark for success, some children will always fail.

Principle 2: Every child has potential that may not have been exhibited up to this point.

It is unrealistic to expect schools to provide the opportunity for children to fulfill all of their potential. What is realistic is to expect schools to offer students the opportunity to realize their potential in some areas. Areas of potential include the following:

- Creative potential (visual arts, music, drama)
- Intellectual potential
- Physical potential
- Academic potential
- Social potential

It is important for parents and schools to explore all areas to see where a child's true potential lies. Academic success is just one area of potential.

Principle 3: Confidence is the necessary foundation for feeling good about oneself and one's ability.

Like adults, children need to learn that building confidence is something that develops from successful experiences and not overnight. Failure forces a child into a box labeled *inadequate*. Coaxing a child out of this box is not easy, but a child can become self-confident if teachers and parents recognize the difficulty the child has faced previously and nurture the child's hope that change is possible.

Principle 4: Once children have confidence, they will be motivated to try other experiences.

Success breeds success. However, it is important for children to realize that different people gain confidence at different rates. Achieving a sense of self-confidence is not a competition but a process that unfolds in all children.

Principle 5: Feeling confident and good about oneself is always better than feeling inadequate.

Children who lack confidence learn over time to perceive their feelings of inadequacy as a "normal state"—normal for them, at least. They must experience success to learn that feeling good about themselves is better than feeling inadequate.

As a parent, you are in charge and know what you are doing. Being a good "lifeguard" is crucial in helping your child feel secure and confident. Conveying a strong leadership message gives your child structure and the understanding that you care enough to try to nurture his or her potential.

GUIDELINES FOR PARENTS   **Number 1**

Many factors contribute to a child's self-confidence—for instance, the influence of the peer group or previous school performance. Parents can't possibly control all these factors, and neither can teachers. However, as a parent you can help off-set negative influences on your child's self-confidence by considering the following guidelines and taking the ones you feel are helpful to heart.

Become introspective about your own issues and how they affect your parenting.

If when you evaluate your own self-esteem you experience feelings of inadequacy, changing your child's feelings about him- or herself will be more difficult. Increasing your child's self-confidence is a process that needs to be viewed in a positive way. The more you can work to resolve your own issues, the better you will be able to help your child.

Be solution oriented.

An important step in building your child's self-confidence is to teach solutions rather than assign blame. In some families, when something goes wrong family members are quick to point the finger at one another. Teaching solutions instead of blaming begins with simple statements like "Who's at fault is not important. The more important question is, What can we do so that it doesn't happen again?" A problem-solving orientation gives children a sense of control.

Preserve your child's right to make decisions.

Despite what some children would like, families are not democracies. However, giving your child the right to make decisions that affect his or her daily life enhances self-confidence.

Making decisions about clothing, room arrangement, friends to invite to a party, the menu for dinner, and so forth gives your child a sense of self-control.

Offer alternative ways of handling a problem situation.

Some people know only one or two ways to handle a problem situation. After these fail, they become frustrated. Teaching your child to seek many alternatives for handling problems enhances self-esteem and builds confidence. Ask your child what he or she has tried, and provide guidance toward other possible solutions.

The next News Note will include more suggestions for helping your child build confidence at home.

Creating Confident Children Parent News Note

GUIDELINES FOR PARENTS   **Number 2**

The last News Note offered a number of guidelines to help build your child's confidence at home. If you've tried any of these suggestions, you may have noticed some improvement in your child's attitude or behavior. If you haven't noticed big changes, don't worry: It takes time to build confidence. The more consistent you are in following the guidelines, the more likely it is that you'll see improvement.

Please consider the following suggestions in addition to those described in the last News Note.

Teach your child the proper labels for feelings.

Children may have difficulty communicating because they lack the emotional vocabulary to label their feelings. When your child is unable to label a feeling, his or her frustration may show itself as a behavior problem or a physical symptom (headache, stomachache, and the like). Offering the correct label gets to the real issue. For example, you may want to say, "You say you are angry, but you also might feel *frustration*. Frustration is feeling upset that you can't do something or get something right. Now that you know this, is anything causing you frustration?"

Allow children the opportunity to repeat successful experiences.

Whenever possible, give your child the chance to handle any job or responsibility in which he or she has already been successful. Cooking dinner, cutting the lawn, fixing something around the house, and making a shopping list are some at-home jobs your child can repeat.

Allow avenues for disagreement.

Children with high self-confidence feel they have a way to communicate their dissatisfaction. Children with low self-confidence tend to believe no one will listen if they express disagreement. Even though the result may not be in your child's favor, the knowledge that you will listen to a disagreement will help your child build a sense of purpose.

The next News Note includes some final suggestions for you to consider.

GUIDELINES FOR PARENTS   **Number 3**

Most busy parents find it difficult to juggle job and basic family responsibilities like getting dinner on the table or kids in the bathtub. However, confidence building is cumulative. That means putting some of the suggestions in this and the previous two News Notes into action can have a positive effect on your child's performance at school as well as on his or her attitude at home.

Here is the last group of guidelines for you to think about.

Help your child define objectives.

Ask your child what he or she wants to accomplish and help map out the steps to define the task. Each step becomes a goal in itself. At every step, your child has the opportunity to succeed and feel a sense of accomplishment.

Help children set realistic goals.

Realistic goals are crucial in building confidence. Unrealistic goals result in failure, and repeated failures may cause your child to set more unrealistic goals or refuse to take chances. The more limited your child's experiences, the less likely his or her opportunities for success. Gently question any goals that seem unrealistic.

Use a reward system to shape positive behavior.

Punishment tells a child what not to do, whereas *rewards* tell a child what to do. Rewarding positive behavior builds confidence. Rewards can be a special snack, time alone with you, a later bedtime, a hug and a kiss, or just your words of appreciation for your child's effort or achievement.

Don't pave all your child's roads.

Some parents (and some teachers!) make the mistake of reducing frustration for children to the point where the child receives a distorted view of the world. By rushing to the aid of your child, you may be reinforcing your child's belief that he or she is incapable of handling the situation alone. After a while, your child may become dependent upon you for a "bailout" whenever a situation is frustrating. Frustration, if not too intense, can help your child build tolerance to situations that don't work out exactly as he or she would like.

CHARACTERISTICS OF CONFIDENCE

Confident children seem to share certain characteristics. In their relationships with both teachers and parents, they show in many ways that they are empowered, hopeful, autonomous, resilient, and secure. They also are accomplished, receive recognition for their accomplishments, and persevere even when things don't go as they would like. Finally, they genuinely seem to enjoy life, both at school and at home.

A list of these characteristics follows, along with a few suggestions for what you might do at home to create an atmosphere to nurture them.

- **Empowerment** is being given the authority or power to act as you wish. Give your child choices whenever possible—of the dinner menu, bedtime, what TV show to watch.

- **Hope** is desire accompanied by the expectation of fulfillment—the genuine belief that things will work out as you want them to. Within reason, grant your child's wishes (for example, for a birthday present or a special privilege). Remark on other situations in which something the child has hoped for has come to pass.

- **Autonomy** is the belief that you have the ability to govern yourself. Give your child the tools he or she needs to function independently. For a younger child, this might be a step-stool to reach the sink. For an older child, this might be an alarm clock or a bus pass.

- **Resiliency** is the ability to bounce back from unsuccessful experiences. Be available and supportive when your child experiences a setback. Point out times your child has bounced back successfully before, or give examples from your own or someone else's life that illustrate the rule "Two steps forward and one step back."

- **Security** is the quality or state of being free from danger, fear, or anxiety. Set schedules for mealtimes, bedtimes, and other family routines. As much as possible, follow through on what you say you will do, and try not to make promises you can't keep.

- **Accomplishment** is the sense that you have brought something about by your own efforts. Give your child lots of praise for making an effort, as well as for achieving a final outcome or reaching a certain goal.

- **Recognition** means receiving special notice or attention. Be on the lookout for ways your child is unique, and tell your child and the rest of the family about what you notice. Celebrate successes frequently, whether they are big or small.

- **Perseverance** means to pursue a goal in the face of difficulty, discouragement, or opposition. Encouragement is the key here: Tell your child you know he or she is trying hard, and praise even partial success.

- **Enjoyment** is taking pleasure and satisfaction in what you do. Take the time to schedule activities you know your child enjoys—even better if the whole family can do something fun together.

About the Authors

Dr. Roger Pierangelo has over 30 years of experience as a regular classroom teacher, school psychologist in the Herricks Public School System (New Hyde Park, New York), administrator of special education programs, professor in the graduate Special Education Department at Long Island University, private practitioner in psychology, member of committees on special education, evaluator for the New York State Education Department, director of a private clinic, and consultant to numerous private and public schools, PTA, and SEPTA groups.

Dr. Pierangelo earned his B.S. from St. John's University, M.S. from Queens College, Professional Diploma from Queens College, and Ph.D. from Yeshiva University. Currently, he is working as a licensed clinical psychologist in private practice, school psychologist, teacher at the graduate level, and director of a private clinic.

Dr. Pierangelo is the author of numerous books, including *The Survival Kit for the Special Education Teacher* and *The Special Education Teacher's Book of Lists* (Simon and Schuster). He is coauthor of *The Parent's Complete Guide to Special Education, The Special Educator's Complete Guide to Transition Services, and The Special Educator's Guide to 109 Diagnostic Tests* (Simon and Schuster); *The Special Education Yellow Pages* (Merrill); and *Why Your Students Do What They Do and What to Do When They Do It* (*Grades K–5* and *Grades 6–12*) and *What Every Teacher Should Know About Students With Special Needs* (Research Press).

Dr. George A. Giuliani earned his B.A. from the College of the Holy Cross, M.S. from St. John's University, J.D. from City University Law School, and Psy.D. from Rutgers University.

Dr. Giuliani is a licensed psychologist with an extensive private practice focusing on marital counseling, individual psychotherapy, and children with special needs. He is a member of the New York Association of School Psychologists, New York Psychological Association, and the National Association of School Psychologists. Dr. Giuliani is involved in early intervention for children with special needs and is a consultant for school districts and early childhood agencies. He has provided numerous workshops for parents and teachers on a variety of psychological and educational topics.

Dr. Giuliani is coauthor of *The Special Educator's Guide to 109 Diagnostic Tests* (Simon and Schuster), as well as *Why Your Students Do What They Do and What to Do When They Do It* (*Grades K–5* and *Grades 6–12*) and *What Every Teacher Should Know About Students With Special Needs* (Research Press).